The GREAT OUTDOORS

SEASHORE

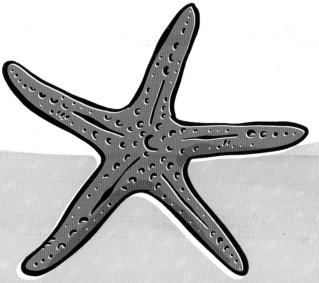

LISA REGAN

WAYLAND
www.waylandbooks.co.uk

First published in Great Britain in 2019
by Wayland
Copyright © Hodder and Stoughton, 2019
All rights reserved

Created for Wayland by www.squareandcircus.co.uk
Design and illustrations: Supriya Sahai
Editor: John Hort

HB ISBN: 978 1 5263 1101 6
PB ISBN: 978 1 5263 1102 3

Printed and bound in China

Wayland, an imprint of
Hachette Children's Group
Part of Hodder and Stoughton
Carmelite House
50 Victoria Embankment
London EC4Y 0DZ
An Hachette UK Company
www.hachette.co.uk
www.hachettechildrens.co.uk

The website addresses (URLs) included in this book were valid at
the time of going to press. However, it is possible that contents or
addresses may have changed since the publication of this book. No
responsibility for any such changes can be accepted by either the
author or the Publisher.

Picture credits: All images Shutterstock: Brian Kinney 4a; JennyMB
4b; David Ionut 5a; Ruslan Gubaidullin 5b; simone tognon 6a; Ethan
Daniels 10a; Greg Amptman 12a; Adnan Buyuk 12b; LABETAA
Andre 12c; bluehand 12d; scubaluna 12e; feathercollector 13a;
Krasowit 13b; Arunee Rodloy 13c; GOLFX 13d; Re Metau 13e;
NatalieJean 14a; Dmitry Rukhlenko 14b and 16a; haraldmuc 14c;
Damsea 14d; Bildagentur Zoonar GmbH 14e and 20d; Aleksey
Stemmer 14f; BW Folsom 14g; Simia Attentive 14h; itor 15a;
Vagabondivan 15b; SNC Art and More 15c; bonchan 15d; Lia_Skyfox
17a; Brandon B 18a; J Need 19a; Julian Popov 20a; Eric Isselee 20b;
Enrique Aguirre 20c; francesco de marco 21a; Fotopixel Norway
21b; RealityImages 21c; Brian Lasenby 21d; Julian Popov 21e; Petr
Simon 21f; Pyma 22a; Aerial-motion 22b; Pawel Kalisinski 23a;
FiledIMAGE 23b; Leonardo Gonzalez 23c; Michael Smith ITWP
23d; Neirfy 23f, PARFENOV1976 23e; ben bryant 24a; Olaf Speier
24b; Harry Wedzinga 24c; CTatiana 24d; Rudmer Zwerver 25a;
Wut_Moppie 25b; IvanaJankovic 25c; Martin Fowler 25d; kzww
25e; Marcel Pietersen 26a; Christian Musat 27a; Guido Montaldo 27b;
Brian Hanchett 28a; Take Photo 29a; wim claes 29b.

Every attempt has been made to clear copyright. Should there be any
inadvertent omission please apply to the publisher for rectification.

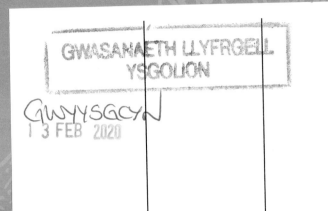

CONTENTS

WHAT IS A SEASHORE?

The land at the edge of seas and oceans is known as the seashore. You might see sand dunes, towering cliffs or a sloping beach that leads into the waves. Some of the land will be covered at high tide, and then exposed when the tide goes out.

What can you see?

There are different types of beach and seashore for you to explore.

Sandy beaches are covered with small grains of finely ground rocks and shells. They may be white or golden brown, but can be pink, green or even black.

DID YOU KNOW?
Places near the sea are described as **coastal habitats**.

Shingle beaches have small pebbles instead of sand. They often slope more steeply than sandy beaches, with ridges that show the level of the tides.

Rocky beaches can look very dramatic, with caves and arches found next to sheltered coves. The sea pounds against the rocks and **erodes** them to form new shapes.

Muddy beaches are often found at the **mouth** of a river. Plants may grow here, as long as they can live in salty soil and water. **Mangroves** and **salt marshes** are types of muddy coastline.

Colourful coral forms reefs in warm, shallow salt water along some of the world's coasts.

ON THE BEACH

A day at the beach usually involves fun in the waves, digging in the sand and building sandcastles. Have you ever wondered what makes waves and sand, and why damp sand is the best for building with?

Making waves

In the open ocean, the water moves forward in a constant pattern of waves. They are caused by the wind passing across the water's surface. As the waves reach the shore, the shallow waters cause **friction** between the seabed and the water. This slows the water at the bottom of a wave, allowing the faster water at the top to rise higher and form the breaking waves that surfers love.

A wave breaks, or collapses, when it becomes too high for its width to support it.

Smaller and smaller

Rocks are tough, but over the course of thousands or millions of years, they can be broken into smaller pieces by oceans and the weather. They become rock fragments, decreasing in size until they turn into pebbles and eventually sand. Some beaches also have grains made of ground-up coral and shells.

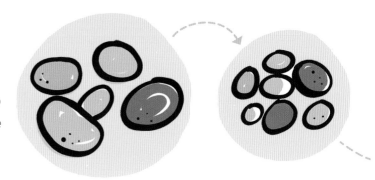

Wave formation

The highest part of a wave is called the crest. The lowest part is called the trough. The face is the front of a wave.

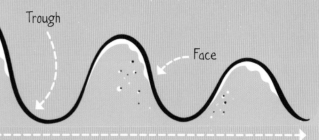

Crest

Trough

Face

Direction of travel

TRY THIS...

MAKE STICKY SAND!

With the right ingredients, you can make your own version of the sticky sand that you find in toyshops.

- Pour 4 cups of clean sand (as fine as possible; play sand is the best) into a large bowl. Add 2 cups of cornflour. Mix them together.

- Pour in 1 cup of water, a small amount at a time, and mix. It should hold together when you squeeze it into a ball, without being wet.

- Mix in 2 tablespoons of powder paint to make your sand colourful. Use your hands to thoroughly mix all the paint into the sticky sand.

- Store it in an airtight container.

Building with sand

If you've ever made a sandcastle, you will know that dry sand falls apart, but wet sand sticks together. The water molecules in the wet sand are attracted to each other and hold the sand in shape. If you add too much water, though, the sand is too **diluted** to stay in place, and simply trickles away.

TIDES AND TIDAL ZONES

Seashore creatures and plants are specially adapted to survive in salt water, and to the changing conditions created by the ocean's tides. Tidal zones are home to many small and simple **organisms**.

High and dry

The area that is covered by water only during high tide is called the <u>high tide zone</u>. Here, you will mostly find creatures with shells. Below that is the <u>middle zone</u>, which is covered and uncovered with every tide. This is where most sea creatures are found. Even lower down is the <u>low tide zone</u>, which is exposed only when the sea goes out a long way at low tide. The creatures here tend to be soft-bodied and vulnerable to predators.

Mussels

Kelp

Sea cucumber

Anemone

Sea star

Urchin

Snail

The spray zone or splash zone is rarely under water but gets wet when large waves break or during storms.

SPRAY ZONE

Periwinkle

Limpet

Barnacles

HIGH TIDE ZONE

Crab

Brittle star

MIDDLE TIDE ZONE

Sea lettuce

LOW TIDE ZONE

Tides

The gravity of the Moon pulls the ocean back and forth to give us high and low tides every day.

Twice in each month, when there is a new Moon and a full Moon, the low tides are lower and the high tides are higher than normal. This is due to the Sun's gravity working with the Moon's gravity. These are known as spring tides.

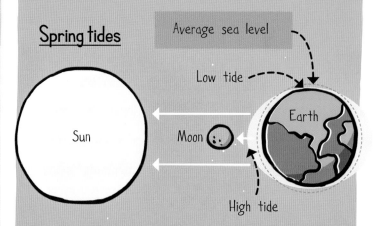

Spring tides

Average sea level

Low tide

Sun

Moon

Earth

High tide

Seven days later, when the Moon appears half-full, we get neap tides. Now, low tide is higher, and high tide is lower than normal, as the Sun's gravity and the Moon's gravity are working against each other.

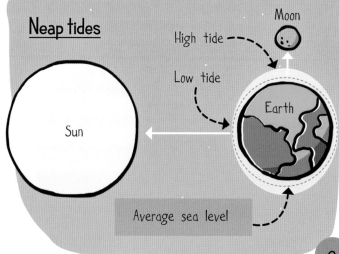

Neap tides

Moon

High tide

Low tide

Sun

Earth

Average sea level

ROCK POOLS

At low tide, pools form where the retreating ocean leaves water in hollows among the rocks. They are called rock pools, or tide pools. They can be small and shallow or large and deep, and are home to all sorts of **algae** and animals.

REMEMBER:

Only explore a rock pool with adult supervision, and always wear non-slip shoes.

Don't get caught by the incoming tide.

Never disturb or remove anything you find.

Warm water

The water in rock pools is heated by the Sun and is warmer than the ocean.

Limpet

A mussel's shell has two parts, hinged together.

A sea urchin's spines fall off when it dies.

Sea palm

Seaweed is not truly a plant, but is a type of algae.

Blenny

DID YOU KNOW?

Although sea anemones look like plants, they are actually animals. They have a hollow central column with a mouth at the top, and lots of stinging tentacles for catching prey. They are full of muscles that allow the anemone to move and change shape. Underneath, they have a hard disc which acts as a sticky foot and keeps them anchored in one place.

TRY THIS...

MAKE A ROCK POOL VIEWER

Any of these devices will help you to see more clearly if there are ripples on the surface of the rock pool.

- Use a large, clear plastic lunchbox. Hold it just under the surface of the water and look through the bottom.

- Remove the lid from a large milk carton. Cut the bottom out of the milk carton. Hold it near the bottom of the pool and look through the small opening as an eyepiece.

- Find a wide piece of pipe, like a drainpipe offcut. Cover one end with a tightly-stretched clear plastic bag. Hold it in place with extra strong duct tape. Point the covered end at the bottom of the pool and look into the top of the pipe.

Sea stars often have five arms, although some types have more.

Winkle

Prawn

Goby

Crab

Pipefish

Sea sponges have been on Earth for at least 500 million years.

Sea anemones are animals, although they look like plants.

11

SEASHORE FISH

Many fish stay in the deeper waters, but there are plenty that swim close to shore or live in rock pools. Sometimes you will see their shadow on the sea floor before you see the fish themselves. Keep your eyes peeled!

Pipefish

Long and very skinny, with a pointed snout, these striped fish are members of the seahorse family. They are poor swimmers so often live in the shallows.

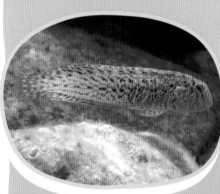

Blenny

Sometimes known as a shanny, this is a small, slimy fish that hides under rocks and sometimes lies on seaweed at the side of a pool, before plopping back into the water if it is scared.

Goby

Rock gobies and common gobies are long, slender fish that dart here and there in shallow waters.

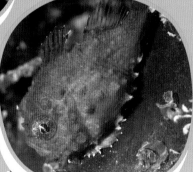

Lumpsucker

Lumpsuckers have specialised fins underneath which form a sucker so they can stick to rocks. They live mostly on the seabed.

Mullet

These fish are often seen swimming in a harbour in large groups, changing direction together as they flit to and fro. They also live in muddy estuaries.

Snailfish

Similar in appearance to a giant tadpole, these fish have no scales. They burrow into the mud and sand on the sea floor.

Stickleback

Its name comes from the spines along its back. It is a tiny fish with sharp teeth, and it hides in seaweed to catch its food.

Wrasse

They often come in a wide range of bright shades and beautiful patterns. Corkwing and ballan wrasse are generally brown. Look for them in rock pools.

TRY THIS...

Seahorse

Seahorses live mostly in shallow, warm water. They rest by wrapping their tail around seagrass.

TURN SALT WATER INTO FRESH WATER

Taking the salt out of seawater is called desalination. Try it for yourself!

- Place a cup in the middle of a bowl or lunchbox. Pour seawater into the bowl until it is halfway up the cup.

- Cover the bowl with clingfilm, sealed tightly around the edges. Place a pebble on the clingfilm over the cup.

- Leave it in full sunshine while you play in the sand.

- After a few hours, you should have fresh water in the cup, and a layer of salt inside the bowl.

Flounder

These well-camouflaged flatfish feed in the soft mud of a river mouth or in shallow seas.

LIFE IN THE SAND

Seaside creatures can be found in the sand as well as in the water. Many of them burrow beneath the surface to stay cool and wet when the tide is out. Some leave telltale signs for you to look for.

Feeding holes

Soft-shell clam
Sometimes known as sand gapers, these clams bury themselves in the mud. At low tide you might see the holes they make for feeding.

Cast

Lugworm
The spaghetti-like casts of these worms are more easily seen than the worms themselves. The worms are red, and are often dug up to use as fishing bait.

Edible crab
The edible crab has a reddish-brown shell with a pinched, scalloped edge, a bit like the crust of a pie.

Sea star
Sea stars used to be known as starfish but have been renamed as they aren't fish at all; they are related to sea urchins.

Test

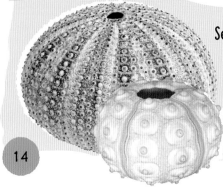

Sea urchin
Under the water, sea urchins are spiky, like a hedgehog. You may find their beautiful discarded hard shells (called tests) on the beach.

Anatomy of a crab

A crab is a decapod, meaning it has ten legs. It uses eight of these for walking. The front two legs are the claws and are used for feeding. A crab's mouth is on its underside. The shell on top is tough and is called the carapace. A crab sheds its outer shell as it grows, so you may find an empty one on the beach.

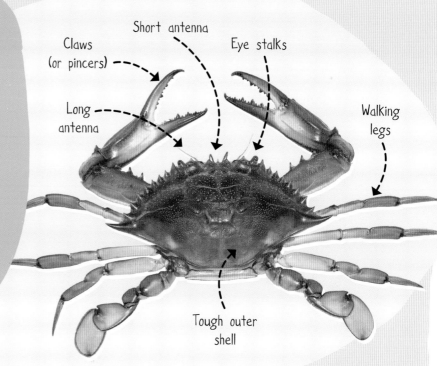

Claws (or pincers)

Short antenna

Eye stalks

Long antenna

Walking legs

Tough outer shell

Razor clam

Razor clams have long and slightly curved shells (in Europe) and shorter, oval shapes (in North America). They have two-part, hinged shells but you might only find one half in the sand.

Sand mason

This worm makes its own home from bits of shell and sand glued together with mucus. These little tubes stick up above the sand like candles on a cake.

Hermit crab

A hermit crab has a soft body and no shell of its own, so it crawls into an abandoned shell for protection. As it grows, it leaves one shell to move into a larger one.

SHELL SEEKERS

Many of the shells you find on the beach will be empty, but some will contain sea creatures. Shells are home to all sorts of **molluscs**, including oysters, mussels, clams and snails. Be sure to put them back where you found them if there is a creature living inside.

Building a home

A mollusc has a soft body and often needs protection from its surroundings and from predators. Some molluscs create their own shell from minerals and can make it bigger as they grow. These minerals are mostly calcium carbonate, formed by taking in chemicals from the sea water.

Different diets

A mollusc's diet affects how its shell looks. Warm-water molluscs, like this nautilus, tend to eat a wider variety of food than cold water molluscs, making their shells brighter and more colourful.

The nautilus

Soft body

Hard shell

Univalve molluscs

Univalve molluscs have a single shell. They are known as **gastropods** and have a foot and a head that can extend outside of the shell. They come in different shapes. Limpets and cowries are univalves with a conical shell. Whelks, periwinkles and conch have a rounded spiral shell. Auger shells are pointed and spiral.

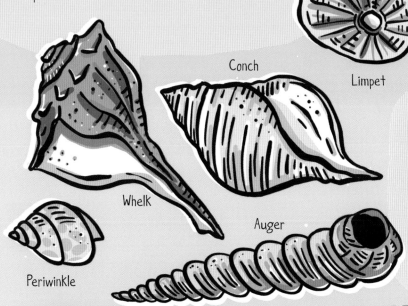

Cowrie

Mussel

Oyster

Cockle

Limpet

Conch

Whelk

Periwinkle

Auger

Bivalve molluscs

These molluscs have shells made of two parts. They are joined with a hinge so they can open and close to find food. Mussels, cockles, scallops, oysters and clams are all examples of bivalve molluscs.

TRY THIS...

MAKE A PIECE OF ART

Gather together empty shells to make your own beach art.

- Arrange your shells in symmetrical patterns to make an abstract piece.
- Make a sand sculpture in the shape of a mermaid or a turtle, and use shells to decorate it.
- Write your name, your location and the date using shells.
- Save your shell art for ever by taking a photo.

BE CAREFUL

It can be illegal to take shells home with you if you are on a trip abroad. Nor should you buy any shells, or items decorated with shells, as souvenirs.

SEARCHING FOR SEAWEED

Seaweed looks like a plant, but it is actually a type of algae. Seaweed often has fronds that look like leaves, but it doesn't have roots. Instead, it has **holdfasts**, which keep it anchored but don't gather **nutrients** like a plant's root does. Like plants, seaweeds take in sunlight to make food, using the process of **photosynthesis**.

Underwater forest

Seaweed can cover large areas and is very important as it provides the oxygen we need to breathe. During photosynthesis, the seaweed absorbs sunlight and uses it to change carbon dioxide and water into sugary energy. Oxygen is given off as a by-product.

The largest seaweed is giant sea kelp that grows to 60 m long. It grows up to 30 cm per day!

Sea sorrel

Wakame

Dulce

Brown seaweed is found in cold oceans and on rocky shores. Some brown seaweed is edible, such as kelp and wakame. Others, such as sea sorrel or acidweed, taste nasty and can cause a stomach upset. Bladderwrack has pods of air on its fronds to keep it floating upright in the water.

Red seaweed can grow in the deepest waters, but is also found near the shore. Some types are used as an ingredient in foods, including ice cream, bread and sushi.

Green seaweeds include sea lettuce, which is a popular food for people.

Sea lettuce

Bladderwrack

TRY THIS...

Not seaweed!

Sea fir and hornwrack are not seaweed, although they have fronds and look similar. They are both made up of collections of tiny animals. Goose barnacles gather on rocks and can also be mistaken for seaweed, but are actually crustaceans . If you find a leathery mermaid's purse, you are actually holding the egg case of a dogfish or a ray, which once had a baby fish inside it.

Mermaid's purse

GO BEACH COMBING

The ocean washes up many treasures. Some of them are best captured in a photo, but some can be taken home. Always respect nature and your surroundings.

- Driftwood is beautiful and you are allowed to remove small pieces that are not embedded in the sand.

- If you want to collect pretty pebbles, choose just one and keep it as a memento.

- Any other manmade objects can be taken home with you. Look for pieces of glass that have been smoothed by the sea.

  (While you're at it, why not fill a rubbish bag with waste, and take it home to put in a bin?)

SEA BIRDS

Many species of bird feed and nest on the seashore. Some of them make their home on the steep cliffs, where their eggs remain undisturbed by predators. Others hide their nest in the grass on marshy land.

Common tern

Silvery wings, a black head and a bright red beak make these birds easy to spot. In flight, look for their distinctive forked tail.

Out to sea

Some sea birds hardly ever return to land. These **pelagic** birds, including albatrosses, frigatebirds and shearwaters, can soar for weeks and even sleep in the air. Others, including terns, gulls and pelicans, feed at sea but rest on dry land.

Gannet

This yellow-headed bird circles in the air and then dives into the water to catch fish.

Herring gull

These large gulls make a loud noise that sounds like a laugh or a shriek.

Oystercatcher

These noisy birds lay their eggs in hollows on stony ground. They use their long orange beak to smash open shells to eat the creature inside.

Shearwater

These birds spend a long time out at sea, and can often be seen following fishing boats, looking for fish and scraps.

DID YOU KNOW?

If you watch seabirds flying overhead, you will notice that they don't flap their wings very often. Instead, they have long, thin wings that allow them to glide. They use air currents, caused by the land and ocean waves, to keep them aloft. Some use rising air, pushed up by the cliffs, to climb high in the sky.

Puffin

Small, with a brightly striped triangular beak, a puffin has short wings that help propel it underwater.

Pelican

The most noticeable part of these large birds is their huge beak and stretchy throat that can expand like a bucket for catching and holding fish.

Turnstone

These birds can be seen using their slightly upturned beak to turn over stones and seaweed, looking for creatures to eat. They line a hollow in the ground with leaves to make their nest.

Kittiwake

Listen carefully for these birds, as their name echoes the call they make. Large colonies of them nest on cliffs.

Cormorant

Cormorants and their relatives the shag are large seaside birds that can often be seen standing with their jagged-edged wings held open wide to dry them out.

BEYOND THE SHORE

Some ocean-going creatures never come on to land, but can be seen in the distance or on boat trips. Others spend much of their time in the water, but leave the waves to breed, as seals and sea lions do, or lay their eggs, as turtles do.

DID YOU KNOW?

As well as camouflage, cephalopods have another way of hiding from predators. When under attack, they squirt a cloud of dark ink from their body. Then they escape before the predator has a chance to catch or chase them.

Clever creatures

Squid, octopus and cuttlefish are a type of mollusc known as **cephalopods**. They are much cleverer than most molluscs, with good eyesight and a large brain. They can also camouflage themselves by changing the pattern of their skin to match their surroundings.

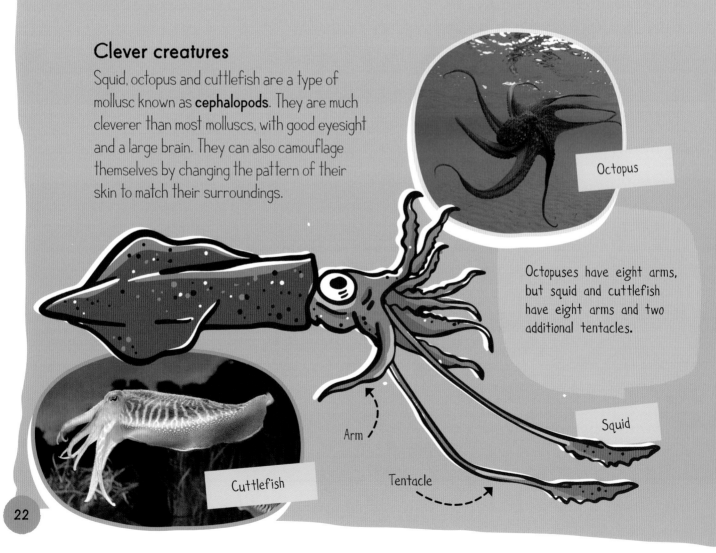

Octopus

Octopuses have eight arms, but squid and cuttlefish have eight arms and two additional tentacles.

Squid

Arm

Tentacle

Cuttlefish

Jellyfish

Also called sea jellies, as they are not actually fish, these are a common sight on many coasts. Look out for them on the beach or floating in the water. Many can give you a painful sting.

Seal

Seals leave the water to **moult** and give birth. Sometimes they sleep on dry land. They gather in large groups on secluded beaches.

Porpoise

These animals are related to dolphins but have a shorter, more rounded snout.

Sea lion

Sea lions are larger and can walk on land better than their relatives the seals. They twist their back flippers to use them like feet.

Sea turtle

There are seven species of sea turtle, all protected by a shell. They use their flippers to swim, and to swipe jellyfish into their mouth.

Dolphin

There are over 30 species of dolphin, and they mostly feed on fish and squid. They are mammals, so have to come to the surface to breathe at regular intervals.

GRASSES AND FLOWERS

It can be hard for plants to grow at the seaside. They have to be tough enough to survive strong winds and salty sea spray. Coastal soil can be poor, with high levels of salt and sand, and low levels of nutrients.

Sea pink/sea thrift

A common sight in salt marshes and on cliffs, this plant can cope with dry, sandy, salty soil.

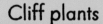

Samphire

Different varieties of this grow around the world. Each has different coloured flowers, but most have fleshy, edible leaves.

Cliff plants

The steep sides of a cliff allow most of the soil to fall away, leaving little for a plant to put its roots in. Most cliff plants have long roots to hold on tight, and are short and bushy so they don't get buffeted by the wind.

Sea lavender

This plant is well adapted to salty soil so is commonly found on the coast.

Ice plant/Hottentot fig

This low-growing plant can survive in strong winds. It covers large areas, like a carpet.

Sand dunes

Sand blows up the beach until it hits an obstacle such as a rock, driftwood, or a plant. Then it is deposited, and gradually builds up to form a slope called a sand dune. If plants such as grasses can put down strong roots, they help to hold the dune together.

Sea holly

These amazing blue flowers are surrounded by spikes, and grow taller than many seaside plants.

Marram grass

The roots of this plant help to hold sand dunes together. Its leaves are sharp enough to hurt your legs as you walk through it.

Sea rocket

The flowers of this plant attract bees and butterflies. Its very long roots hold it firm in the sand.

Wild cabbage

Related to broccoli, cauliflower and edible cabbage, this leafy seaside plant has fleshy leaves that help it to store water.

SEASHORE FOOD CHAIN

The plants, animals and algae that you find at the seaside all interact with each other. They form food chains, which link together to form a food web. A food chain shows what is eaten by what; for example, a fish is eaten by a dolphin.

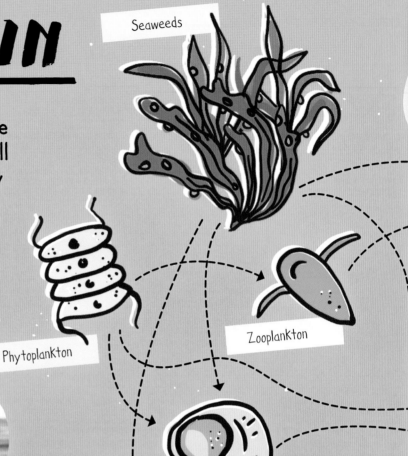

Seaweeds

Phytoplankton

Zooplankton

Periwinkle

Limpet

First in the chain

The first living thing in a food chain makes its own food from the sun. On the seashore, this can be a plant, algae (or seaweed) or plant **plankton**. These **producers** are then eaten by primary **consumers**, such as limpets or **zooplankton.** These are in turn eaten by secondary **consumers**, such as crabs and seabirds. A food chain can contain many consumers.

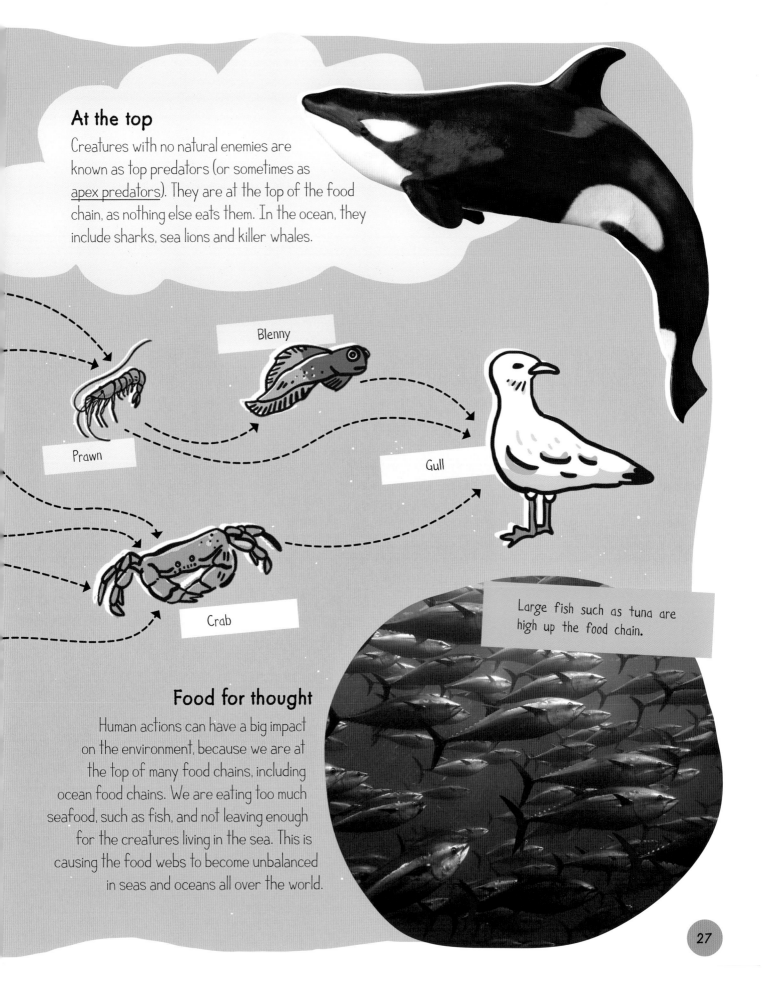

At the top

Creatures with no natural enemies are known as top predators (or sometimes as <u>apex predators</u>). They are at the top of the food chain, as nothing else eats them. In the ocean, they include sharks, sea lions and killer whales.

Blenny

Prawn

Gull

Crab

Large fish such as tuna are high up the food chain.

Food for thought

Human actions can have a big impact on the environment, because we are at the top of many food chains, including ocean food chains. We are eating too much seafood, such as fish, and not leaving enough for the creatures living in the sea. This is causing the food webs to become unbalanced in seas and oceans all over the world.

PROTECTING OUR SEASHORES

The coast is a constantly changing landscape. Cliffs are worn away by the ocean and the weather, and sand dunes come and go with the wind. However, humans are also making a big difference — and not always in a good way.

Rising sea levels

Human activity such as the burning of fossil fuels has led to climate change, which is resulting in an unnatural rise in the level of the oceans. This leads to an increase in erosion, large storm surges and flooding of areas close to the coast. Wildlife habitats are lost, and thousands of people's homes are destroyed.

Plastic pollution

Every year, millions of tonnes of plastic ends up in the ocean and on the seashore. It pollutes the water and is dangerous to sea life. Scientists find thousands of creatures that have died by getting tangled in plastic, or by eating it.

Coastal soil erosion

Danger zone

All kinds of nasty things can end up on the beaches and in the ocean: sewage, chemicals from farms and factories, and even oil from damaged oil tankers. They harm the wildlife and make the beach a toxic, unsafe place.

Spilt oil clings to a bird's feathers so it cannot fly.

Coral bleaching

Coral reefs are one of nature's most beautiful and precious creations. They form a natural barrier against storms and floods, and are home to a huge range of living things. However, when coral is stressed, by changes in temperature or light, it turns white and is vulnerable to disease.

HOW CAN YOU HELP?

You can play a part in making the seashore and oceans cleaner and safer.

- Always take your litter home with you after a day at the beach.

- Recycle plastic bags and other waste so it doesn't end up in the sea, and reduce the amount you buy in the first place.

- Join an organised litter pick to tidy up your local beach.

Only eat fish that has been caught **sustainably**, as overfishing is a threat to ocean food chains.

In 2005, the US lost half of its coral in the Caribbean because of an increase in temperature.

QUIZ

1. A shingle beach does not have sand. What is it made up of instead?

a) Mud
b) Pebbles
c) Seaweed

2. Where do most soft-bodied and vulnerable creatures live?

a) The splash zone
b) The high tide zone
c) The low tide zone

3. Anemones look like plants, but are actually what?

a) Animals
b) Algae
c) Fish

4. Which fish has modified fins which help it stick to rocks?

a) Seahorse
b) Blenny
c) Lumpsucker

5. What helps seabirds to glide without flapping their wings for long durations?

a) Solar power
b) Air currents
c) Tidal waves

6. Which clever molluscs can use camouflage to hide from predators?

a) Cephalopods
b) Arthropods
c) Decapods

7. A sea lion has no natural enemies. What kind of predator is it?

a) Apex
b) Convex
c) Complex

8. What effect do rising sea levels have on coastal areas?

a) Eradication
b) Erosion
c) Eruption

ANSWERS: 1b, 2c, 3a, 4c, 5b, 6a, 7a, 8b.

GLOSSARY

algae (singular = alga) a non-flowering organism, usually growing in the water

cephalopod a mollusc with tentacles attached to its head, such as an octopus or squid

coastal found where the land meets the ocean

consumer in a food chain, a creature that eats plants or other creatures

crustacean a mostly aquatic group of creatures with a hard outer shell

diluted made thinner by adding water

erode to slowly wear something away or grind it down

friction resistance caused by one thing moving over another

gastropod mollusc with a one-piece coiled shell, such as a snail

holdfast a root-like part of seaweed that attaches it in one place

mangrove a tidal swamp with trees whose roots are exposed at low tide

mollusc an invertebrate with a soft, unsegmented body

moult to shed hair, feathers, shell, horns, or an outer layer

mouth the lower end of a river where it flows into the ocean

nutrient a substance that provides essential nourishment for living and growing

organism a living thing, such as bacteria, plants, or animals

pelagic birds that live on the open sea

photosynthesis the way plants and algae produce food

phytoplankton microscopic plants that drift in the sea

plankton microscopic organisms floating in the sea; see phytoplankton and zooplankton

producer the first part of a food chain, consisting of plants, plankton and algae

salt marsh land that is wet or flooded with seawater

shingle lots of small, rounded pebbles

sustainable keeping the balance of nature (by avoiding taking too much)

INDEX

FURTHER READING

These websites and books will give you lots more ideas about the great outdoors!

www.wildlifetrusts.org/about-us

www.fsc-uk.org/en-uk

www.woodlandtrust.org.uk/naturedetectives

www.rspb.org.uk/fun-and-learning/for-kids
  facts-about-nature

www.nationaltrust.org.uk/children-and-nature

hwww.discoverwildlife.com

www.fws.gov/index.html

Habitats (Science Skills Sorted!)
Anna Claybourne (Franklin Watts, 2019)

Illustrated Compendium of the Sea
Virginie Aladjidi (Franklin Watts, 2016)

Ocean Life (Visual Explorers)
Paul Calver and Toby Reynolds (Franklin Watts, 2019)

Rivers and Coasts (Geographics)
Izzi Howell (Franklin Watts, 2018)